A Note to Parents

DK READERS is a compelling program for beginning readers, designed in conjunction with leading literacy experts, including Dr. Linda Gambrell, Director of the Eugenge T. Moore School of Education at Clemson University. Dr. Gambrell has served on the Board of Directors of the International Reading Association and as President of the National Reading Conference.

Beautiful illustrations and superb full-color photographs combine with engaging, easy-to-read stories to offer a fresh approach to each subject in the series. Each DK READER is guaranteed to capture a child's interest while developing his or her reading skills, general knowledge, and love of reading.

The five levels of DK READERS are aimed at different reading abilities, enabling you to choose the books that are exactly right for your child:

Pre-level 1: Learning to read
Level 1: Beginning to read
Level 2: Beginning to read alone
Level 3: Reading alone
Level 4: Proficient readers

The "normal" age at which a child begins to read can be anywhere from three to eight years old, so these levels are only a general guideline.

No matter which level you select, you can be sure that you are helping your child learn to read, then read to learn!

LONDON, NEW YORK, MUNICH,
MELBOURNE, AND DELHI

Senior Art Editor Cheryl Telfer
Designer Sadie Thomas
Series Editor Deborah Lock
Editorial Assistant Fleur Star
U.S. Editor Elizabeth Hester
Production Shivani Pandey
DTP Designer Almudena Díaz
Jacket Designer Chris Drew
Photographer Zena Holloway
Consultant Rick Cross

Reading Consultant
Linda Gambrell, Ph.D.

First American Edition, 2004
04 05 06 07 08 10 9 8 7 6 5 4 3 2
Published in the United States by DK Publishing, Inc.
375 Hudson Street, New York, New York 10014

Published in Great Britain by Dorling Kindersley Limited

Library of Congress Cataloging-in-Publication Data
Wallace, Karen.
I can swim! / by Karen Wallace.-- 1st American ed.
p. cm. -- (DK readers)
Summary: George becomes increasingly confident as his father
teaches him to swim in a pool.
ISBN 0-7566-0274-2 (HC) -- ISBN 0-7566-0273-4 (PB)
[1. Swimming--Fiction.] I. Title. II. Series: Dorling Kindersley
readers.
PZ7.W1568Iag 2004
[E]--dc22
                                  2003016716

Color reproduction by Colourscan, Singapore
Printed and bound in China by L Rex Printing Co., Ltd.

Photographs taken at Charing Cross Sports Club,
with thanks to Richard Walsh and Perry Marks.
Thanks also to all the models: Tim Pilcher, Jack Lofthouse,
Emma Lofthouse, Rochea Brown, Max Moore, Shaym Patel
Jack Lofthouse is a member of the
Water Nippers Swimming Group

Discover more at
www.dk.com

DK READERS

BEGINNING
1
TO READ

I can swim!

Written by Karen Wallace

DK Publishing, Inc.

George's friends laughed
and splashed around.
Swimming looked like fun!

George stood by the pool.
His dad was going to teach him
how to swim.
Dad helped George to put on
his water wings.

water wings

"Let's get in," said Dad.
George held onto the ladder
and stepped into the pool.

ladder

He splashed his face
and put it into the water.
"Good job!" cried Dad.
"You'll be a great
swimmer one day!"

George stood in the shallow water
and jumped up and down.

He walked back and forth.

Then Dad held him
while he floated on his back.
"That was fun," cried George,
as he climbed out of the pool.

At their next lesson,
Dad helped George move
through the water on his front.
"Kick!" Dad said.
George kicked with long,
straight legs as hard
as he could.

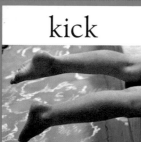

kick

Dad showed George how
to put his face underwater.
He held on to the side of
the pool, then took a deep
breath and ducked.

George watched him
blow bubbles like a fish.
"Now you try," said Dad.

fish

Next, George took lots of
deep breaths and blew a ball
across the water.
"Good breathing!" cried Dad.
"Next time, you can try
to paddle."

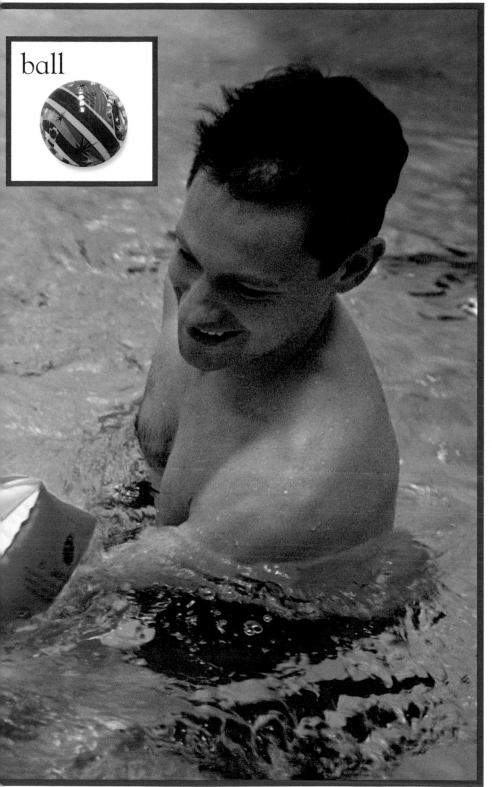

ball

"Can you remember what you've learned?" Dad asked at the next lesson. George thought about how to kick and to breathe.

paddle

Dad showed him
how to paddle
and pull back with his arms
through the water.
George tried paddling.

George learned to push
and glide on his front.
He held onto a kickboard and
stood by the side of the pool.
Then he pushed off with
his feet and glided through
the water.

kickboard

"Let's take some air out of your water wings," said Dad. George tried floating like a starfish.

starfish

First he took a deep breath.
Then he lay on his back.
He spread his arms
and his legs out wide.

Then George pushed off
from the side on his back.
He glided across the water.
"Push harder this time," said Dad.
"You'll glide even farther."

George pushed off
as hard as he could.

Each time George went to the pool, he practiced his new skills. One day, Dad said, "It's time to take off your water wings."

George tried to paddle
without any water wings.
Soon he could use his arms
to pull through the water.

"Now hold out your kickboard," said Dad, "and kick your legs." George tried.
"Try not to splash," said Dad. "You'll go even faster."

George tried hard.
Soon he could swim across
the pool without using
the kickboard.

Mom came to the pool
to watch George.

"I've got a surprise
for you," said George.
He swam across
the pool to her.

"I can swim!" shouted George.
Mom cheered and clapped.

Some of George's friends
were swimming in the pool.
George swam over
to play with them.
Now he could swim, too!

Picture word list

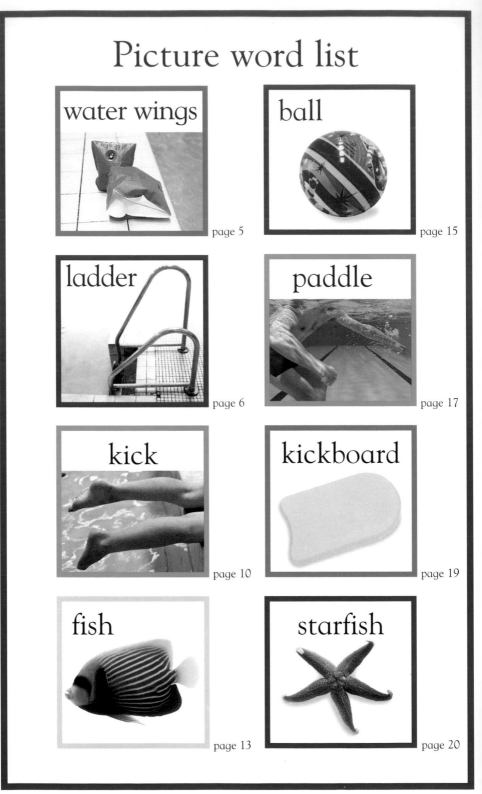

water wings
page 5

ball
page 15

ladder
page 6

paddle
page 17

kick
page 10

kickboard
page 19

fish
page 13

starfish
page 20